SIMPLE LOVE DIALECT

REVEALING THE HIDDEN TRUTH TO LONG-LASTING LOVE

BY

LARRY J WILLIAM

TABLE OF CONTENTS

Catalog

DESCRIPTIONS

what kind of inquiries may couples make during their date evenings to deepen their connection

to one another better.?

depending on how long the couple has been married and how h

they've communicated in the past, different questions might apply to various couples. This book is written by **LARRY J WILLIAMS** and we will be talking about things and languages that are encouraged to use for both an existing or a romantic relationship that is about to begin and some simple ways to keep it in love for a very long time.

CHAPTER 1

LOVE IS A DECISION

IS LOVE A SENSATION OR A DECISION?

It is challenging to give a clear answer to this issue. There isn't a single page in a single book that will inevitably have the answer. There isn't a single magical article or guru who has all the answers. And it's all right! The specifics of this query will be covered in this book.

You've probably heard a couple say they're breaking up because they're just no longer feeling the passion. We love each other, but we aren't in love with each other, they might even say. You may have even caught yourself doing this in the past.

But remaining in a relationship is a choice. It's not only an emotion, as most people believe, and you may choose to do it.

What Is Said About Romance and Relationships in the Media and Popular Culture?

Romantic comedies almost always have the same resolution. Between the person she was with at the start of the movie and the person she has met along the road, the girl must make a decision. She comes to the realization that this new person is the one for her at some point in the film, and that the sentiments of love she felt for the first person are no longer present (or never really were). Much of this has to do with how love is portrayed in society and the media as an action rather than a choice, which it isn't.

It might be simple to believe that you are no longer in love with the other person if you are going through a lot of difficulty in your relationship or if you feel like you have simply grown apart.

We are aware that we might be feeling differently than we did previously in real life as well. Long-term love relationships end because one or both partners decide they are simply no longer experiencing the love, unaware that they have the option to choose to feel this way.

Periods of Love

We simply don't comprehend what love truly is—that it is a choice, not a feeling—which is one of the reasons why so many people feel as though they are no longer in love.

Many people believe that the first sense of love is something that the other person can give to them. This is interpreted as the butterflies in their stomach, the thrill that makes their pulse skip a beat, and all of the other early signs of a union between two people. A new romantic relationship or exciting life event triggers a physical and chemical reaction in the brain that results in these experiences. Whether we want to let these feelings of love in or not, they will come.

WHAT EXACTLY IS LOVE, ANYWAY?

People assume that the reason why these signs and symptoms of love start to go away is that they thought they were experiencing love when they weren't. However, in romantic relationships, this is very acceptable. It is normal for every love connection that will survive for a long time to experience this unavoidable feeling of change. This is because the brain adjusts over time and stops releasing the same high quantities of feel-good neurotransmitters.

Each stage of love has distinct phases that relationships go through. If a couple were to be in that initial stage of love all the time, they would not be able to achieve in other aspects of their lives. There is only one person you can think of. You have them on your mind from the moment you wake up until you fall asleep. Without even making a conscious decision to feel this way, you want to spend all of your time with them. This kind of love is impossible for anyone to maintain indefinitely. It's natural for your love relationship to grow and your sentiments for your partner to evolve as time goes on.

Another myth is that there is a perfect match for every person. This is often referred to as a soulmate. As a result, when a romantic relationship becomes challenging, people assume that they just made the incorrect choice. They then begin to believe that their true love is still undiscovered and waiting for them.

When a person's thoughts begin to shift in this direction, they immediately begin to hunt for a means to end their present romantic engagement. Why should I continue in this relationship when my soul mate is still out there? they ask themselves.

We have the power to make relationships work because there isn't one individual who is right for everyone. Imagine how many people would not be with the proper person if this were true. The entire world of relationships may be thrown off if just one person made the incorrect choice.

That is not how it operates. The choice is yours as to who you dedicate yourself to, but the truth is that we are all capable of loving different people.

Love relationships are challenging because they involve two distinct individuals who may have divergent opinions. It is not because you are not married to your soul match that your relationship is difficult. Because you are a human, it is.

Perceiving things as being better on the other side of everything

Every couple faces challenges, but nobody wants to make that fact known to outsiders. Therefore, it is sometimes common to plaster on a grin and try to make our relationship look wonderful in front of other people rather than discussing their relationship narrative. This has been made worse by social media content, which solely displays highlight reels.

You begin to believe there is something wrong with your relationship when you are continuously surrounded by what you perceive to be perfect love partnerships. Why do you argue all the time when everyone else is so content? Why does her spouse bring flowers home for her but not yours? Why does your girlfriend not continuously praise you online while his girlfriend does?

In romantic relationships, it's risky to play the comparison game. It is simple to decide to believe that the other person is better and that your love connection would be simpler and better if you were just with them. However, it is not because the grass is greener if you observe a love connection that is more successful or fulfilling than your own. It is a result of the couple's decision and ongoing relationship work.

Love is difficult, and romantic partnerships demand effort. The people who appear to be doing well are either concealing their issues or making a conscious decision to develop their romantic relationships. Choose to begin improving your love relationship rather than choosing to end it in favor of something you believe will be simpler. You'll soon find yourself back in the same situation if you break up with your love and try to find someone easier to be with.

HOW TO CREATE TRUE ROMANCE THAT WILL LAST FOREVER

YOU CAN'T POUR FROM AN EMPTY CUP, SO PAY ATTENTION TO YOURSELF.

Make sure you're doing what you need to in order to be well and happy in order to boost your love relationship. It's crucial to understand that both parties in a love relationship have the capacity to decide to improve things. It might be simple to overlook the little things our partner performs to maintain our love relationship, and occasionally we undervalue when we have erred. The decision to maintain a love connection depends heavily on open communication and a readiness to listen. Decide to start talking about what you both could do differently if you want to have a successful relationship.

GET HELP IMMEDIATELY

Don't worry if you're hesitant to seek out professional assistance from a therapist. Love relationships can be incredibly challenging, and many couples eventually seek couples counseling.

A therapist will be able to assist you to identify the problematic areas in your romantic relationship and provide solutions. They will assist you in developing crucial communication skills that can shorten and simplify disputes. Additionally, they can aid in rekindling your relationship and bringing back the original motivation for your union. A therapist can still create a "treatment" plan that helps you improve your current relationship even if you are generally satisfied with it.

Love is not a natural phenomenon that lasts forever. You must devote time to your relationship if you want it to endure. You should put every penny of effort into it because it will be worthwhile.

CHAPTER 2

DISCOVERING LOVE

Movies would have us believe that when we think of falling deeply and quickly in love with someone, some huge romantic gesture will be what finally kills us. However, the truth is that everyday, insignificant occurrences frequently constitute indicators of falling in love. Pay attention to any changes you've made to your regular routine that might be a sign that, in contrast to other partners you've dated in the past, this one (this partner, this relationship) might be unique.

According to scientists, when you are deeply in love, your brain enters a particular state. This means that brain scans that display the regions of the brain that are most active differ noticeably from scans taken before or after a breakup or when you're not in love. We turned to the experts because, unlike a Target run, we can't just drop in for a brain scan to confirm if we're falling for someone (or not).

few indicators that you're falling in love have been compiled here by relationship specialists.

YOU'RE PARTICIPATING IN (AND APPRECIATING) YOUR SPOUSE'S HOBBIES

Have you purchased unusual equipment and accessories for a new hobby your partner introduced you to? You may be starting to fall in love. People in relationships who attempt new interests together can keep the spark alive even after the honeymoon phase has passed, according to experts cited in a 2008 New York Times article. The operative word here is "new." According to Arthur Aron, a professor of social psychology, couples should plan their date nights around the novel and enjoyable activities rather than returning to the same old haunts and dining with the same old acquaintances.

YOU'RE SINGING EVERY LOVE SONG ALONG

Dopamine, adrenaline, and norepinephrine, feel-good neurotransmitters, put you in a cheerful frame of mind (so there's no need for sad songs anymore) when you fall in love, so you can find yourself humming along, even to tunes you don't like. In a statement to Science Daily, Pat Mumby, Ph.D. claimed that "falling in love triggers our body to unleash a rush of feel-good chemicals that induce certain physical reactions."

PAIN IS ALMOST MEANINGLESS

You did read that correctly. According to research, even just looking at a picture of a loved one can drastically lessen moderate discomfort by 40%, according a 2010 Stanford University School of Medicine study. According to Sean Mackey, M.D., the study's author, "There are major changes in people's mood that are altering their experience of pain while they are in this passionate, all-consuming phase of love."

YOU'RE MORE CONCERNED WITH YOUR PARTNER'S CONTENTMENT

It's true love when you can put their feelings above your own.

A strong, long-term relationship is characterized by compassionate love, or the capacity to empathize with your spouse. "One should expect spouses who love each other compassionately to stay together longer, be happier, and support one other more effectively than couples who do not love each other compassionately," say marriage experts at UC Berkeley.

YOU'RE INTERESTED IN WHAT THEIR FRIENDS SAY ABOUT YOU

You might be falling in love if you start to show concern for your friends, plan group hangouts, and inquire about your significant other's impressions of you after a date. According to Mara Opperman, a relationship etiquette expert, "by making the effort to get close with your S.O.'s friends, you are showing your S.O. how much you care about them."

YOU'RE DRAWN TO THEIR WEIRDNESS

If habits that typically upset you don't, there's another indication that you might be in love. In fact, you might even find them cute in a way. Don't be afraid to be yourself because we all have different preferences and a person's quirks can actually make us love them more. "The same thing you're trying to keep from them is what will connect with you, get them to open up to you, and make them like you," "Your vibe changes when you have a sense of passion, and you light up from within," is another justification for being genuine.

YOU APPEAR MORE ANXIOUS THAN USUAL.

A Psychology Today article claims that there is a link between the stress hormone and falling in love. As enjoyable as it may be, data suggests that experiencing love is associated with greater levels of the stress hormone cortisol (Marazziti & Canale, 2004). Therefore, if you're feeling worried, tight, or jittery for no apparent reason, it may be a typical reaction to the stress of frequent social interactions with someone whose opinion matters a lot to you.

YOUR HEART SKIPS A BEAT OCCASIONALLY.

According to science, when you are in the presence of someone you love, your heart rate increases.

THEIR FRAGRANCE IS ACTUALLY SEDUCTIVE

According to experts, scent can play a significant role in attracting people to you, and we might even have a great scent match.

It's the cause of things like wanting to wear their old T-shirt to bed or liking the way your bedding smells when they first wake up.

YOU DON'T FEEL AS HUNGRY

Perhaps it's because you have butterflies in your stomach.

One tiny study of a sample of men conducted by researchers at Harvard Medical School and published in the journal Obesity suggests that oxytocin, also known as the "love hormone," may also act as an appetite suppressant in addition to being a "feel-good" chemical.

THE FUTURE IS FREQUENTLY RAISED

such as the wedding six months in the future and your holiday plans. It implies that you desire a lasting relationship. The fact that you have already overcome that annoying hurdle suggests that love is in the air because many people are afraid to talk about the future.

IT'S INCREDIBLY SIMPLE.

In other words, you don't need to overthink everything as you did in previous relationships. You can simply "be" with that person when you're with them

YOU FREQUENTLY DISCUSS THEM.

It can even start to annoy relatives and friends a little, but since it's endearing you get away with it (it might have something to do with those feel-good hormones we talked about in your brain)

YOU DESIRE CONNECTION

We're not saying you have to be hip-to-hip with your partner, but you do want to be aware of their whereabouts and how their day is going.

Serena Gold-stein, a naturopathic physician in New York City, claims that even a brief separation from your partner is similar to coming down from a high. According to Gold-stein, anxiety, and depression are exacerbated when we are separated from our partner because the eutrophication-releasing factor is elevated as a result of the stress response. This could be the reason you have such a strong desire to communicate, especially with long-distance partners. According to the CNN report, one strategy long-distance couples use to manage this stress response is to become addicted to their partner's voice.

CHAPTER 3

KNOWING YOUR MAIN LOVE LANGUAGE

WHAT TYPES OF INQUIRIES MAY COUPLES MAKE DURING THEIR "DATE EVENINGS" TO DEEPEN THEIR CONNECTION AND GET TO KNOW ONE ANOTHER BETTER?

Depending on how long a couple has been married and how they've communicated in the past, different questions might apply to various couples.

I created something called Love Talks for Couples, a small flip board with a different question on each page, about a year ago. I believe that inquiries like these would be appropriate for a date night.

What distinguished your family from others in your area or the families of your friends as you were growing up?

What do you recall from your driving lessons? There are many things that could come out of that, including information on your personality or your parents' personalities.

Can you remember going to your parent's place of employment? If so, explain your experience there.

You can see how these queries might go in a variety of directions. None of them are meant to cause a fight between a couple. They are inquiries meant to help people get to know one another.

Here's one more:

"Fill in the blank: I'm sure my parents wished I would... "

Your response to that query may indicate something about your personal disappointment or your perception that you have let your parents down.

Which movie do you think was the worst you've ever seen?

Name your preferred elementary or secondary school instructor.

There are also a ton of other questions. You want to chat about topics on date nights that you might not normally discuss in the course of a typical day, in my opinion. These Love Talks for Couples are a perfect example of a small item that can sometimes be very effective in igniting dialogue between the two of you.

You should not air your complaints at this time. A date should be entertaining. Marriage intimacy has to do with disclosing and sharing oneself. One of the questions was, "Tell me your most serious bodily injury as a youngster," and I recall going over them one evening with my wife and my buddy Raymond Preston, who assisted me in putting them together.

A date should be entertaining. Marriage intimacy has to do with disclosing and sharing oneself.

My wife told me about the incident in which she got into the medicine cabinet when she was five years old, took a number of sleeping tablets, and slept for 36 hours. It was a terrible problem, and the doctors were attempting to figure out what was wrong with her. She had never told me that during our forty years of marriage. She said, "I wasn't trying to hide anything; there was just never a good time to convey that."

If there was nothing to spark the conversation, these kinds of inquiries encourage couples to open up and share personal information about their history, present, and future.

WHEN YOU NO LONGER EVEN LIKE YOUR PARTNER AND FIND IT CHALLENGING TO EVEN BE IN THE SAME ROOM WITH THEM, HOW CAN YOU POSSIBLY LOVE THEM?

Even though it's a poor scenario, many couples are there. We should, in my opinion, approach that honestly. The Five Love Languages has this as one of its advantages. Because the foundation of the love language theory is that love is a feeling, not a sensation. But you'll start to feel something if you do fall in love.

Love in the Bible is not an emotion. The mentality of "I chose to watch out for your interests" is love. How may I be of service? A style of thinking and acting is love.

The good thing about this is that your partner starts to feel appreciated when you do show love, especially when you do so in their primary love language. And you start to feel good about them when they start using your love language.

Love can be expressed without warm sentiments being present. It's crucial that you decide to love your partner. I believe this is the reason the bible commands husbands to love their wives. The elder women are obligated to teach the younger women how to love their husbands, according to

Titus 2.

Love is not an emotion if it can be ordered, taught, or otherwise acquired.

There's a good chance that emotional warmth will be revived in that marriage even if I don't feel in love with my spouse but I understand God wants me to communicate my love to them and I'm willing to embrace that attitude and have suitable behavior. A commitment is a way of thinking about life, a declaration of my intention to keep my word. When the sentiments are gone in a marriage, it is definitely more difficult because I am no longer being propelled along by my emotions as I was before the marriage. My feelings may even be pulling me on the wrong path. However, because I did make a vow, I won't merely continue my marriage. The goal is to continue being married while taking steps that could improve your relationship.

My decision to show my husband love has the potential to strengthen our marriage.

WHAT ACTION IS MOST IMPORTANT FOR A COUPLE TO TAKE WHEN MENDING A BROKEN MARRIAGE?

Trust to me is like a delicate plant. When a person stops trusting their spouse, it's because they have been dishonest and have betrayed that trust. It is comparable to walking on that plant.

It's similar to trust. Because we've made a commitment to one another and entered into marriage with each other's trust, trust stands tall in a marriage. Until one of them proves untrustworthy, trust will continue. The tiny plant stoops down when that occurs.

The small plant will straighten out if the offender will confess their sin, turn away from their wrongdoing, and then start living honorably once more by following through on their commitments. And the marriage will give new life to trust.

My decision to show my husband love has the potential to strengthen our marriage.

When confidence is repeatedly betrayed, it's as if the plant has been severed. Although you can no longer see the plant, the roots of faith are still present. When a person repeatedly betrays their spouse's trust, it frequently happens in a marriage.

The only way for trust to be reborn is for the person who betrayed the trust to decide to be trustworthy, regardless of where they are, whether it is the first time or many times. and as a result, alter their way of life so that they follow through on their commitments.

Giving the spouse proof that you are now trustworthy is one approach to do this. For instance, if a husband betrayed his wife by being unfaithful to her, it's possible that he started an emotional or even sexual relationship with someone else. Later, he apologizes, begs for pardon, and swears to remain true to her.

How is he supposed to convince her? How will her trust develop? As he shows her that he will keep his word, her faith in him will grow.

I'm going to George's place tonight to work on his car, let's assume he tells her that. She phones George's home an hour later to see whether her spouse is there. She's checking on me, the husband exclaims. That's right, and that's good, is my response. Her faith in you increases each time she calls and discovers that you are acting as you promised and that you are in the location you stated.

However, if she calls and discovers that you didn't fulfill your promise, her trust in you will start to wane once more.

A person must develop their level of trustworthiness in order for trust to be reborn. The person must possess some proof of their reliability in order for the confidence to increase.

If your spouse calls to confirm that you are acting as you promised, if you have truly changed, and if you are truly dedicated to them, you should not disagree. Because of what they are doing to reestablish your trust, you should be happy.

CHANGING LOVE LANGUAGES OVER TIME

IS IT FEASIBLE FOR LOVE LANGUAGES TO ALTER OVER MARRIAGE, OR DO OUR EXPECTATIONS ACTUALLY CHANGE?

An individual's love language doesn't, in my opinion, alter with time. I believe it is formed early in life and persists throughout our entire lives. In a marriage, though, we might believe that our Love Language has changed.

Sometimes it's because we misdiagnosed our love language or our spouse's love language the first time. On occasion, we leap to conclusions without fully understanding the situation.

For instance, it happens frequently for men to declare, "My And because their sexual needs have not been adequately addressed during the marriage, they instantly declare that they would feel loved if their needs were met. However, if their sexual demands are satisfied, they may one day realize that's not their preferred love language. "Words of affirmation are my love language," or something like that.

When a man's physical requirements are not addressed, his demand for sexual fulfillment takes precedence over his need for emotional love. As a result, many men misidentify their love languages.

The fact that a person's primary and secondary love languages are so closely related may also lead one to believe that their primary love language has changed. Love Language is physical touch," after reading my book on the **SIMPLE LOVE LANGUAGES.** If that's the case, your secondary love language will take on greater significance once your primary love language has been sufficiently satisfied.

Couples should consider it a great benefit if their spouse has two love languages that are roughly comparable. They will feel good about either of those options. So you should concentrate on both of those.

Using Your Husband's Love Language

How can ladies effectively prepare the way for their husbands to serve as the household's spiritual head? I frequently get asked that when I am speaking to couples. There is a lot of hazy thinking on both the husband and wife's parts regarding a husband taking the initiative to be a leader (or spiritual leader).

In a book I authored a few years ago titled Five Signs of a Loving Family, I revisited the five cornerstones of a strong family. The husband's role as a caring leader is one of the essentials found in the Bible. This is a basic problem in happy families; it is not a side issue. All five of those, incidentally, are taken from Ephesians 5 and 6, the section on marriage and family.

I included a chapter on how ladies might support their husbands in being the head of the home and in the community in that book. Men respond favorably to praise, which was another point I mentioned in that chapter. Because he is bothered by the typical woman who wants her husband to develop into a loving leader. She's criticizing him by pointing out things he ought to be doing.

I advise her to look for something that he is doing well. Something that demonstrates leadership and confirms it for him.

As an illustration, I'll occasionally ask a lady who is whining about her husband's lack of leadership, "Tell me, does your husband have a solid job?" And she does so frequently. I respond, "So he brings home money on a regular basis to help support the family and pay the mortgage? You know, according to the Bible, that's a very significant step. According to the Bible, a man who doesn't provide for his own family is worse than a non-believer. This leadership is quite significant. A man who is regularly employed, bringing in income, and handling bill payments are taking a significant leadership step. So why don't you concentrate on complimenting him for the labor and resources he offers?"

You can search for affirmation in a variety of other places. Consider the spiritual realm. There is room for praise if he attends church with her on Sunday. The majority of husbands don't attend church.

If a wife were to say to her husband, "Honey, I haven't told you this lately, but I just want you to know how much it means to me, how much I appreciate you, and how proud I am of you to know that you go to church with me every Sunday morning. You may be aware that my friend Mary's husband travels around 50 percent of the time, but my friend June's husband never does. We enjoy going to church together so much.

That husband will leave with a positive self-image and an open mind to personal development. Start praising your husband for any indications of leadership—that's the first step.

The notion that requests produce more results than demands is the second. Of course, whether you're a man or a woman, this is true. Don't place demands on your husband if you want him to develop into a spiritual leader.

You come out as being God and telling your husband what he should be doing when you say things like, "You ought to be reading bible tales to the kids." or, "You ought to be praying with these kids at night."

Is it acceptable for a lady to praise her husband before asking him to do something, such as saying, "You know honey, would it be feasible for you to read the bible story to Johnny tonight? I must complete the dishes. She is specifically asking him to act in a certain way. And if he does, it will be proof of his spiritual leadership.

Making demands, and the more precise the request, the more a wife will urge her husband to be a spiritual leader.

Some wives, I know, will argue that it won't mean as much if I have to beg their husbands to do something. We are all in the process, let's face it. Your hubby might still have a ways to go. You might have to wait a while if you wait for him to consider what he needs to do in order to be a spiritual leader. We are discussing a wife who supports her husband in his role as a spiritual leader. Maybe if he came up with it himself, you'd get 100 emotional points of encouragement. Give him at least 50 points and express your satisfaction that he complied with your request with 50% confidence. And a husband will eventually learn how to perform such things.

SUITABLE BOUNDARIES

WHAT RULES DO YOU RECOMMEND FOR SETTING GOOD BOUNDARIES WHEN PUTTING YOUR SPOUSE'S NEEDS BEFORE YOUR OWN?

Fundamentally, we must acknowledge that every one of us has spiritual, bodily, social, and emotional needs. The Bible commands me to serve my wife and dedicate my life to her, just as Christ did for the church. When a wife submits to her husband, she does it with the same attitude. The phrase "submit yourselves to one another" comes before both of those words. Additionally, wives are advised to submit to their husbands, and husbands are counseled to love and devote themselves to their spouses.

Therefore, for the husband and wife, the biblical paradigm of serving your spouse is present. In the same way that Christ took the effort to love the church, I believe the husband should do the same. According to the Bible, we love Him because He loved us first.

In order to give my life to my wife, I must understand that if my physical, emotional, and spiritual needs aren't addressed, I won't always be there to take care of her needs.

I created something called Love Talks for Couples, a small flip board with a different question on each page, about a year ago. I believe that inquiries like these would be appropriate for a date night.

For instance, if I don't take care of my bodily requirements for food, rest, and exercise, I'll pass away before I can offer her my life. She'll be on her own. It is essential to understand that in order to continue serving our spouses throughout time, we must first take care of our own basic requirements in order to remain healthy individuals.

You must schedule daily alone time in the spiritual realm with God. Nothing can replace that private, everyday moment when you and God sit down, listen to God, and spend this private time together every day. You won't serve others as you should and won't be the spouse or wife God meant you to be if you don't regularly meet with God and grow in your spiritual life.

You must schedule time for your emotional requirements as well. We can become so stressed out from all of our activities that we lose our ability to emotionally love our wives. It's crucial to understand your emotional makeup and what you require to maintain emotional equilibrium.

Some people find that taking five-minute breaks throughout the day is really helpful. They only need to go around the house for five minutes to maintain their emotional equilibrium. Different people experience it differently. You must become aware of your own limitations, comprehend the effects of stress, and know when to take a break and focus on your heart, mind, and body.

In order to do what the bible instructs us to do, which is give our life out to one another, taking care of ourselves is essential.

PUTTING YOUR SPOUSE FIRST

HOW CAN YOU ELEVATE YOUR SPOUSE ABOVE YOUR KIDS IN IMPORTANCE?

Theoretically, we are aware of the critical importance of our relationships with our spouses and children. We don't want to put those against one another, in a way. Both the health of our partner and marriage as well as the health of our children are crucial.

However, when children enter the picture, we often find ourselves preoccupied with meeting their demands while neglecting those of the marriage and each other almost unconsciously. Then, after a year or two, we notice that our marriage has suffered. We don't sense a connection to one another. Each of us feels poorly about the other. And occasionally, one of us experiences attraction for someone outside of the marriage.

We devote so much time to the kids that we neglect to properly care for our spouse and the marriage generally.

Before the kids arrive, let's sit down and say to one another, "We're looking forward to this child, but there's a risk that one of us will be so focused on the child we'll forget each other. Let's promise that when this child is born, we will bear in mind that maintaining a solid marriage is the most important thing we can do for this child.

You talk about how you can make time for one another at this point. If you haven't already, it might be a good time to start a date night. Saying "Maybe for three months after the baby comes, we won't have a date night where we go out, but we'll sit down two nights a week after the baby's in bed and we'll give an hour to each other" is the appropriate thing to say at this point. Realizing that everything is connected, you decide on some measures to protect your time spent together: You truly can't separate the happiness of your marriage from the well of your child. When you do, disaster ensues. If the marriage is neglected and the marriage disintegrates, all of your good intentions to devote time to that child's life will be lost since that child will instead grow up with only one parent. That is not a good scenario.

HOW DO I PERSUADE MY PARTNER TO ACCEPT OUTSIDE ASSISTANCE, WHETHER IT COMES FROM A COUNSELOR OR A TOOL LIKE A BOOK OR MARRIAGE CONFERENCE?

Nowadays, books, movies, marital seminars, and therapy are all great resources for assistance. Sometimes those who require help the most are unaware that they require it. They are content with the current state of affairs. They may not find fulfillment in their marriage, but rather in their work, their religion, or other social activities. They don't mind that their marriage isn't developing the way they had hoped.

The other spouse fervently desires a change in circumstances. It frequently happens that one partner will want assistance more than the other.

We have long maintained that we cannot change our marriages. However, the truth is that we do impact our spouses on a daily basis. Are we having a positive or negative influence, that is the question? Let's try to figure out how to influence your spouse for the better.

Usually, when one of us sees that our marriage needs support, we tend to become depressed. We frequently judge our partners, which manifests in our actions and causes us to withdraw.

You must first adopt a good outlook and speak positively if you wish to have a positive influence. Step back from the hurt, discomfort, and irritation and consider: "How can I have a good impact on my spouse

You start praising them for the great actions they are taking. After doing that for a while, you approach them with a request. Not immediately - not before you shower them with praise.

You might even contemplate asking, "How can I be a better husband to you? " before making that request. What could I do this week to support you? You start to approach them and enquire about their needs in order to be of service to them. You are putting into practice biblical values that you would like to see others put into effect.

You make your request of them after you've done that for a while and they see a shift in the way you're responding to them. They are more inclined to agree to your request for outside assistance now that they have observed these changes in you and have a positive impression of you.

CHAPTER 3

LANGUAGES OF LOVE FOR NEWLYWEDS

IS THERE A SPECIFIC HABIT OR ACTIVITY THAT A COUPLE COULD ADOPT DURING THE FIRST YEAR OF THEIR MARRIAGE TO HELP SET THEM UP FOR A SUCCESSFUL UNION?

They could first exchange a marriage book. Each of them would agree to read a chapter, and at the end of the week, they would gather and discuss something they had discovered about themselves. It serves as a means of self-expression. In that situation, it is likely that they will develop during the process.

Second, go to a marriage-enrichment gathering once a year for the remainder of your life. It might be a class in your church, a weekend retreat that your church sponsors, or a weekend seminar that travels to your city. Make a commitment to go to a marriage-enriching event every year. Couples will start off on the right foot if they develop that habit throughout the first year of marriage.

A third option is to have a sharing time once a week during which we each discuss one problem that is bothering us, especially during the first six months of the marriage. You hope your partner would change one thing, though.

Because they are still in the early phases of their relationship, some couples are hesitant to do this. The truth is that when two people get married, they learn things about one another they didn't know before. It can be a small detail, something you hadn't noticed previously, or something that irritates you. There must be a method to deal with these issues constructively and bring about change.

I'd like to suggest this. You both promise to sit down once a week, be vulnerable, and ask each other, "Okay, tell me one thing you wish I would alter that would make things better for you." Prior to answering. The spouse begins by praising their mate in three ways. You don't have to do anything that week if nothing disturbs you.

You're acknowledging that we'll make some modifications in the first year by doing this. is the best way to do it. We won't hold onto all the things that irritate us until one night when we shoot each other with the five things that need to be altered. We have a strategy.

CHAPTER 4

LOVE LANGUAGES

WORDS OF AFFIRMATION: Everyone forms connections in different ways when it comes to relationships. Some people are all about the PDA, while others prefer sharing adoring Instagram remarks for each and every anniversary. Still, others like to give gifts to one another whenever they can. But as it turns out, there are several love languages that these people use to express their emotions.

The five love languages identified by Chapman are words of affirmation, deeds of service, quality time, physical touch, and gifts. These "love languages" express how you feel and express your desire for love.

Taking a (free!) love language exam to determine your love language is the obvious first step in all of this. Knowing your native tongue will help you comprehend your partner's expressions of love and find the best ways to express your own.

This post is for you if you discover that your words of affirmation ranking are high. Here is all you need to know if you or your partner's love language is words of affirmation, from what it means and how to demonstrate it to numerous examples and dating advice.

WHAT DOES IT MEAN IF WORDS OF AFFIRMATION ARE YOUR LOVE LANGUAGE?

As you might have guessed, the focus of this love language is on words. Words of affirmation can be supportive and compassionate, whether they are spoken or written, according to Hope Therapy Center's licensed marriage and family therapist

Jennie Marie Battistin. They frequently acknowledge, pinpoint, and appreciate a person's actions, contributions, achievements, or difficulties.

People that use this love language are great supporters of heart-to-heart conversations and compliments—both giving and receiving. We'll go into more specific instances and ideas below.

According to Dainis Graveris, a licensed sex educator and relationship expert with SexualAlpha and MysteryVibe, "For these folks, words are more essential than deeds."

And contrary to popular belief, affirmation is not a "bad" or "needy" love language, according to specialists. According to Graveris, "those who use this love language are typically the ones that pay attention to and care about the little elements of other people's life."

As someone whose love language is an affirmation, I can attest that a simple "I love you" or compliment makes me squishy as a bug. On the other hand, I usually do things like leave sweet little notes around the house for my husband or send my parents good morning SMS as a way to show them my respect and gratitude. And yes, I am that person who always keeps handwritten notes from the individuals I care about.

WHAT ARE SOME INDICATIONS THAT WORDS OF AFFIRMATION ARE YOUR LOVE LANGUAGE?

According to Battistin, one of the simpler love languages to identify is words of affirmation. In addition to verbally hearing "I love you," Graveris claims that you likely really appreciate hearing the reasons why your lover is in love with you.

Other indications include your appreciation when your lover comments on your new appearance, your enjoyment of selecting the ideal birthday card for someone, and the intensity with which love songs affect you. According to Graveris, you probably also take great pleasure in texting your significant other and/or gushing over them on social media.

On the other hand, having a conversation that is unsatisfying, not receiving verbal praise, thanks, or validation, or hearing nasty remarks are very upsetting to someone who uses this love language.

WHAT ARE SOME EXAMPLES OF AFFIRMATIVE LANGUAGE?

Most people find it relatively easy to learn words of encouragement when it comes to love languages. The following are some things you can say and do to show your lover your love in their

Just tell them you love them.

then describe what you find appealing about them.

Express your feelings to them frequently.

Tell them specifically why you are proud of them, such as how they handled a challenging family holiday or a difficult conversation with their boss.

"I'm so lucky to be with you," you should say.

Congratulate them on accomplishments large and small, such as receiving a promotion or parallel parking successfully.

Compliment their smile, their intelligence, their hair, their dress, their scent, and so on.

Thank them for anything they've done for you or your family.

Learn as much as you can about handwritten cards, and be sure to send your spouse a message on every occasion, including holidays and birthdays.

Leave little notes expressing your love for everything around the house.

Before they go to work, put a note in their bag to motivate them on a significant day.

Send them love letters "just because."

Save the cards and messages people send you because, more often than not, they truly mean what they say.

On their birthday, share a nice photo with a thoughtful remark on social media.

Give them vocal affirmation and praise frequently, particularly when they are having a difficult day.

Compliment them on their clothes, manicure, or the day's unique appearance of their blue eyes.

To let them know you're thinking about them throughout the day, text them.

Tell them what you admire about them and how and why they inspire you.

Point highlight their accomplishments and positive traits as they occur, especially while they're young.

Tell them when they make you feel good (in the bedroom and outside of it), that you are attracted to them, and that you value them.

Even in trying situations, remember to communicate and use positive language. Keep in mind that every word has great power, so always think before you say it.

Avoid criticizing, making unpleasant remarks, and making allegations since insults may stick with individuals and are difficult to forget.

It's crucial to keep in mind that these concepts aren't universal. Some people dislike social media PDA, while others prefer succinct compliments to lengthy speeches. Be patient while you and your spouse try to strike the perfect balance by talking about what you want and need.

WHAT ADVICE WOULD YOU PROVIDE TO SOMEONE WHOSE LOVE LANGUAGE IS WORDS OF AFFIRMATION, WHETHER IT BE YOU OR YOUR PARTNER?

Whether you and your partner speak the same or different love languages, communication is essential in every relationship. Things won't advance or flourish if you can't effectively convey your feelings and emotions.

According to Graveris, the initial stage is to "determine your and your partner's major love language and continually speak that language." Using each other's love languages can actually stimulate growth because they "help us learn how to communicate to our spouse love and how they communicate love," as Battistin puts it. This will not only helps you understand each other's needs better.

Here are some things to remember if one of you speaks "words of affirmation" and you and your spouse have determined your love languages:

WORDS OF AFFIRMATION ARE THE LOVE LANGUAGE OF YOUR MATE.

Quite simply: More significantly, they want you to mean what you say. They want you to use your words to reassure, validate, and encourage them. With words of affirmation as their preferred form of communication, couples may find it simple to recognize phony compliments and remarks, according to Graveris. "My best piece of advice is to always speak from the heart while speaking to your mate. They will recognize your lack of authenticity if you mention odd things or makeup things.

Being sympathetic to their sentiments, giving them encouragement when they're down, and giving them as much thanks or praise as you can all help. Don't assume your lover is aware of your affection; express it to them and do so frequently.

Battistin advises setting a daily reminder on your phone to text them something pleasant or even send them a hilarious meme if you find it difficult to remember to give positive verbal affirmation. Purchase a few "thinking of you" cards and send one to your partner every month, she advises, or get some dry erase markers and write "I love you" on the bathroom mirror. You'll soon find yourself conversing in their tongue.

IF WORDS OF AFFIRMATION ARE YOUR LOVE LANGUAGE:

Your companion needs to hear your words of affirmation if that is your preferred method of communication. Couples frequently speak various love languages, so if your partner is unaware that verbal or written expressions of love are effective for you, they might not think to use them. Additionally, Graveris notes that even if your partner understands your love language, they might not be as skilled at expressing their emotions or paying attention to the little things, so exercise patience and forgiveness.

Feeling valued and understood is critical in any relationship, according to Graveris. Just that it has a much greater impact on those whose love language is affirmation. As a result, words probably strike you a little harder. Therefore, try to explain why what you hear affects you without being defensive. It's possible that they were unaware of the significance of what they said.

Finally, it's crucial to remember that depending on the circumstance, your love language may occasionally alter. If you've had a rough day, you might prefer a hug over a pep talk, or you might want to just spend time with your partner without talking about how you're feeling. According to Graveris, it all comes down to talking to your spouse and both of you expressing what you need at the time.

WHAT IF YOU AND YOUR PARTNER SPEAK DIFFERENT LOVE LANGUAGES?

The good news is that couples do not necessarily need to express love in the same way. It all just boils down to knowing how you individually like to offer and receive love. If your partner's love language is acts of service and they frequently assist you with your jobs or chores, know that this is their natural way of expressing their love for you. It's a common misconception that individuals express love in the same way they want to receive it.

Having said that, Battistin asserts that everyone may, with a little time and effort, learn to speak a new (or another) love language. She advises, "Ask your partner what are the meaningful ways you can show them you love them. As they explain, try not to respond defensively; instead, listen carefully and show interest in learning the solution.

Make it a goal for you and your partner to jointly identify and explore your respective love languages. According to Graveris, if you commit to loving each other in ways that are special to each other, your relationship will be fulfilling and happy in no time. And to be honest, I can support such words.

CHAPTER 5

THE BEST TIME:

You interact with your partner every day. They are the ones you call first thing in the morning and the ones you kiss good night.

But does regular contact with one another indicates a strong relationship? No, not always.

The best approach to make sure your relationship remains healthy and robust is to spend quality time with your partner. This entails doing more than just watching Netflix together or occasionally going out to eat. Both you and your spouse deserve more from your relationship.

What is meant by quality time? It entails uninterrupted time spent with your partner. It's an opportunity for you to get together and converse. Building emotional connection and trust through communication.

Spending quality time also involves physically showing someone you care. Not necessarily through sex (although that's awesome, too!), but rather by holding hands, hugging, caring for, and tickling. These affectionate behaviors will increase mate pleasure, according to studies.

So, how do you and your partner spend quality time together? Here are a few relationship pointers for maximizing your time with your significant other.

1. IDENTIFY THE INDICATIONS

You must develop the ability to spot the telltale indicators that your relationship needs more one-on-one time if you want it to be healthy.

Some red flags include:

You never stop using your phones.

You place a higher priority on your interests or friendships than your marriage.

You don't attend significant events together.

You argue more frequently or have poor connections.

You don't schedule events or go on dates.

You're not content.

If you are going through any of these relationship symptoms, you should realize that spending quality time together can counteract their bad consequences.

2. TRY NEW THINGS TOGETHER

Have you ever wished you could learn a new language or a musical instrument? What about ballroom dancing or skydiving?

Why not involve your partner in these activities rather than seeing them as solo interests and hobbies?

Together, trying new things helps couples to rely on one another for emotional and physical support, which strengthens relationships.

Shared interests foster marital connection, and the Journal of Happiness Studies showed that couples who saw each other as closest friends reported twice as much marital satisfaction.

3. PLAN TECH-FREE PERIODS OF TIME

Your phone is a terrific tool for keeping in touch with friends and family, watching videos, and listening to music. But is your relationship better off without your phone?

Numerous couples "phub" or phone snub, one another. Phubbing, according to studies, can make relationships less satisfying and raise one's risk of depression. Eliminate interruptions while spending quality time with your partner and make it clear that they have your undivided focus to lower those risks.

4. WORK OUT TOGETHER IN THE GYM.

Taking up exercise together is one way you may spend more time as a pair. According to studies, couples who work out together are more likely to stick with their program. Couples exercise more vigorously than they would alone. According to one study, compared to 66 percent of singles, 95 percent of couples who exercise together maintain weight loss.

[

Join a gym, exercise together at home, try couples yoga, go hiking, or get your bikes out. Whatever form of exercise you select, these beneficial activities can enhance healthy relationships.

5. **PREPARE FOOD TOGETHER**

While you go to work in the kitchen, of course, crack open a bottle of wine or turn on some sultry music.

Cooking meals together is one of the finest pieces of relationship bits of advice for spending quality time together when you both have busy schedules.

Try to spice things up by cooking a sophisticated French cuisine or a four-course meal together. This is not only a good way to spend time with your friends, but it also fosters cooperation.

If all goes according to plan, you'll have a romantic dinner for two at home that you made with your own two hands. Even if the meal doesn't turn out as you had anticipated, you will undoubtedly laugh and make new memories with your loved ones.

6. HAVE A RECURRING DATE NIGHT.

Spending quality time together increases a couple's sense of satisfaction and reduces stress.

Include a date night in your weekly schedule as one of the most important relationship tips for a happy marriage.

A weekly date night might make your relationship seem more intriguing and help minimize relationship boredom, according to the National Marriage Project.

Additionally, it enhances your sexual life, reduces the likelihood of divorce, and fosters healthy communication.

Here are some fantastic suggestions for your date night activities:

Have a movie marathon and cozy up on the couch with your favorite films.

Together, play board games, card games, video games, and other creative activities for a fun way to bond.

Recreate your first date by returning to the same eatery and placing the exact same order as you did when you first met. By acting as though you are strangers meeting for the first time, you can spice up your evening and see how hot it becomes.

There is nothing better than taking a trip with the person you love. Arrange a weekend break.

DINNER AND A MOVIE—A TIMELESS COMBO!

Try a new restaurant - Set out on a mission to rate and sample every Mexican eatery, Irish pub, and Italian trattoria in your neighborhood.

HAVE A LENGTHY SEXUAL ENCOUNTER. Intimacy encourages the release of the hormone oxytocin, which is responsible for many wonderful experiences.

FINAL REFLECTIONS

Spending quality time together has countless advantages. Here are just a few examples of how it can support a strong bond:

Enhances intimacy both physically and emotionally

Reduces the divorce rate

It enhances communication.

Cuts down on marital boredom

Bonds bring couples together

Strengthens friendship

Improves health

Reduces tension

ALL OF THESE ARE GREAT REASONS TO START INCLUDING DATE NIGHT EVERY WEEK.

When you set aside special time to spend with your partner, it's simple to have a healthy connection. Find novel ways to be close and connected by doing new things together, making your partner your workout partner, and exploring new hobbies.

These dating advice suggestions will do wonders for your marriage.

GETTING A GIFT

You can both obtain what you need from the relationship if you are aware of your own and your partner's love languages. Here, we will examine the significance of the love languages of giving and receiving gifts for your relationship.

You could either know or have a sneaking suspicion that giving and receiving presents is one of your partner's primary love languages. Alternatively, perhaps giving gifts is your love language and you're trying to find a better approach to express your desires.

According to relationship coach and certified mental health counselor Mark Williams, approaching relationships from the perspective of the love languages is quite fruitful. You may make sure both individuals in a relationship feel supported and seen by learning to "speak" each other's love languages.

It's likely that your partner and you have different love languages. Chapman asserts that it's crucial to learn your partner's favorite language. since it can deepen your love, prevent disputes, and help you understand each other better.

THE LOVE LANGUAGE OF GIFTS

Gift-giving and receiving are likely the love languages that are misunderstood the most. Some people can see it as being ungrateful or as the recipient being preoccupied with goods rather than love. That's not the case, though.

According to Williams, "if gifts are you or your partner's love language, it indicates you feel loved [or that you're displaying love] with a concrete item." "It doesn't matter if it's a 50-foot sailboat or a little trinket from a thrift shop. Either way, the message is the same: I saw this and thought of you. Always on my mind is you.

Williams explains that, in this sense, feeling rather than excess is the actual essence of giving gifts. The present may be more meaningful to someone who uses this love language than to someone who uses a different love language. It serves as a constant reminder that they are loved every time they see it.

Examples of how a person who speaks this love language could show their affection include:

sending flowers to their partner, even if there is no specific event

purchasing their partner's preferred snack item while supermarket shopping
Give your partner a gift certificate to a restaurant they've been wanting to visit. Having a coffee or lunch brought to them while they're at work. Getting their partner tickets to see their favorite musician or artist.

leaving a modest present for their lover to discover when they wake up

LEARN THE LOVE LANGUAGE OF YOUR SPOUSE.

"We frequently communicate with our partners in the love language that we would like to receive, "Williams explains. "Consequently, it is likely that your partner's love language is gift-giving if they purchase you an album two days after you express your passion for a new band or if they acquire you a membership to a magazine they believe you'll enjoy. Observing how your partner responds to gifts is another effective approach to determine if that person speaks to you in terms of gifts. According to Williams, if someone feels humiliated upon receiving a gift, it's probably not their love language. On the other hand, if they show extreme enthusiasm, showcase the item, wear it every day, or brag about it to their friends, they probably feel extremely loved by the gesture.

Asking your partner will reveal whether giving gifts is their preferred method of showing their affection.

How to Handle Your Partner's Request for a Gift

If your partner uses the present love language, even if you don't naturally speak it, it's still crucial to try learning it. According to research, employing a partner's love language can boost romantic feelings and improve relationships.

2. Williams advises "looking at things in your regular life through the lens of gift-giving, just like you put a filter on an Instagram photo." If you frequently pass a bakery on your way home from work, consider the thought that "My partner really feels appreciated when I bring them gifts" and pause there for a treat before returning home."

Williams continues, "They don't have to be big purchases." "and they do not have to be always. They are merely tokens that serve as reminders that you are thinking of them often.

PROTECTIONS FOR THE LOVE LANGUAGE OF GIFTS

An insult will hurt that individual more than it will another if that person's love language is words of affirmation. Similar to this, if your partner expresses love by physical touch and you withheld affection for days, they would become discouraged.

Knowing each other's love languages also equips you with the awareness of ways you could damage your partner, according to Williams. According to Williams, "buying them a gift on an anniversary or special occasion would be deeply unpleasant to them," and "approaching the gift-giving as more of a burden than an opportunity would be hurtful to them."

It's equally crucial to understand that some actions may have a more profoundly negative effect on your partner than others.

Message From Very well

We all speak all the languages to some extent, even if the majority of us have one or two main love languages. It's ideal to speak to our romantic partners in all five love languages—physical affection, quality time, acts of service, pleasant words, and gifts—while prioritizing the language they prefer.

PERSONAL CONTACT:

You can show your lover your love in a variety of ways. You can attend a significant fundraiser to demonstrate your support for them. Simply because you were thinking of them, you can purchase them as a present. When they are having a difficult day, you can squeeze their hand.

One of the five love languages is physical contact, but all five are significant since we all give and receive love differently. Understanding your partner's preferences will help you show your appreciation in the most effective way. Consideration of Touch as a Love Language

If physical touch is your preferred form of communication, you value it above all other forms of expression (such as verbal compliments or gifts).

Keep in mind that physical touch is a love language that encompasses more than just sex, though it certainly plays a significant role in romantic relationships. Hugs, shoulder squeezes, hand holds, and even pats on the back can be equally important expressions of affection.

Don't worry if you're in a non-sexual relationship or can't have sex with your spouse because of something (long distance, postpartum, PTSD). We look at simple ways to touch your spouse, no matter where you are with them physically or mentally. There are both personal and non-intimate touches that can and should be utilized to express your partner's love, despite the fact that this may seem self-explanatory.

By Touching Intimately, Show Love

Most romantic relationships involve sexual displays of affection, but what if you live more than 100 miles apart from your partner? What if you two are holding off on having sex? What if you don't have a sensitive nature? What if experiencing sexual closeness causes you mental strain?

Even if you aren't having sex with your spouse, it is still feasible to learn how to show your love through intimate contact.

Contrary to what you may have heard, a relationship isn't just about the sex. Although it is significant, it is not the sole bodily manifestation of love.

According to Clarissa Silva, a behavioral scientist and relationship counselor, "Physical touch, especially snuggling, releases oxytocin, the feel-good hormone that makes you feel like nothing can hurt you." Along with strengthening the closeness between a couple, hugging strengthens your immune system.

Here are some ways to express close physical affection:

You might believe that kissing must result in sex, but this is untrue. One of the simplest, most powerful methods to express physical affection to your lover is by kissing them. You can kiss their hand, lips, neck, cheek, forehead, and hands. Kissing is or has been used as a sign of respect, greeting, or affection in a wide variety of civilizations throughout history. Kissing is utilized in both romantic and non-romantic relationships and should be given priority.

Who doesn't enjoy seeing a couple strolling along the street holding hands? In public or private, holding hands with your lover is a simple gesture that can instantly release mood-enhancing endorphins. Parents frequently hold their child's hand for both protective and physical closeness reasons. One of the best methods to express physical love to your mate is through it.

Do you cuddle with your significant other as you watch a movie? or as you are lying in bed? If not, you ought to. You might become more emotionally and physically connected to your lover by physically encircling each other. Regardless of whether your partner prefers to be the "big" or "small" spoon, try switching roles or facing each other and see how it makes you feel.

SKIN-TO-SKIN CONTACT—A touch might be sexual or nonsexual and still be intimate. An intimate sign of affection can be tracing your fingertips across your partner's back or neck. You can convey your support for your spouse, your physical attraction to them, and/or your relationship by caressing their hair, hugging the back of their neck, or even touching their bare leg.

You can communicate your love without speaking, without doing the dishes, or going out to purchase a gift if you are in a relationship with someone whose love language is physical contact. One of the simplest ways to be intimate with your partner is through physical touch, which can also foster emotional connection.

DISPLAY LOVE THROUGH INAPPROPRIATE TOUCH

One of the finest methods to create a bridge and strengthen feelings of connectivity is to physically touch your companion. You can give your partner a hug or kiss when they arrive home from work to help reduce the strain of the day. These actions are straightforward but profound.

For couples looking for non-sexual ways to demonstrate physical affection without becoming intimate, several non-intimate touches can lead to intimacy:

Rub your partner's back. Touching someone while they are going through a trying or sad time is a natural reaction, and this type of touch may be just as helpful in a love relationship. Your lover can feel your love and support by having you rub their back or give them a massage. You can massage their hand, arm, or another area of their body. Just make sure you're talking to your spouse about it and that they're okay with it.

SITTING SIDE-BY-SIDE is a simple method to show your lover that you care by being close enough to touch. If you want to express your affection for your spouse when out to dinner or at an event, it's possible that you don't feel comfortable kissing or holding their hand. A non-verbal approach to communicating with your spouse is by touching your feet or hips when you are sitting.

Tickling is a physical manifestation of affection, even if some people may not enjoy being tickled. Uncertain about your partner's opinion of this? You only need to ask. Even if your love language is physical touch, communication is essential to every happy relationship.

Observe how you frequently move physically away from your partner when you disagree or dispute with them. Even though it can be difficult to defuse the tension after an argument, touching your lover can often be the most effective approach to rekindle the relationship.

Most likely, you've heard of the term "makeup sex." Reestablishing physical contact with your partner can indicate that the disagreement is resolved and that both of you have moved on. However, not all couples desire to engage in sexual intimacy after an argument. Holding hands, giving a hug, or even kissing someone can be just as significant.

RELATIONSHIPS OVER LONG DISTANCES: PHYSICAL TOUCH

Long-distance relationships make it impossible to touch hands, kiss, or cuddle; but, video chats have made it possible to feel as though you are together even when you are not.

Body language can be just as crucial as verbal communication if your preferred method of communication is physical touch.

Make sure you give your partner your whole attention when you're talking to them on video chat. Go somewhere peaceful. OFFSET your TV. Make eye contact with them and convey a welcoming demeanor to let them know you are physically present.

Silva advises setting up a video date. Establish a date and time and carry out all other activities as you would if you were in the same location.

Dressing up, setting up candlelight, or making wine or champagne are all examples of how to do this. Do everything you typically would, but with video.

Blow each other kisses, mail them things that physically remind them of you (such as a hoodie, a plush animal, or a sachet of your perfume or fragrance), and talk about physically touching each other are additional ways to demonstrate physical touch from a distance. Long-distance couples should use their imaginations as a powerful tool even though it may not be exactly like the real thing.

Message From Very well

Although physical intimacy is frequently necessary for romantic relationships to flourish, sex isn't the only way to express your love for your partner. You can hold their hand while watching a movie together, put your arms around their waist in the kitchen, or give them a cheek kiss before work.

When it comes to physical touch, often the simplest acts of love have the greatest impact.

ACT OF SERVICE

An act of service is the outward manifestation of a kind deed. One of the five love languages, which are particular ways of expressing love, is this. An act of service is really about someone going above and beyond to significantly assist and support the other person. People feel cared for, safe, and loved in return when others take the initiative to lighten some of their duties and obligations. It takes committed time and effort to perform an act of service, usually in a nonverbal manner. Actions speak louder than words because it is practically manifesting in concrete ways. Examples of various acts of service are shown below. To make sure the gesture will be noticed and appreciated, use creativity and your personal knowledge of the person's unique tastes.

As you go through the list, keep in mind that a charitable deed entails more than just performing home duties, making a grand gesture, or going out of one's way to appease the recipient. It's actually about pursuing a much more subliminal emotional sense where they feel like they can rely on you to watch out for them in both tiny and major situations. Pay attention to their daily activities and look for opportunities to cross items off of their to-do list so you can strike the perfect balance between providing and preventing burnout.

FOR YOUR SPOUSE

Pick up their preferred snack when you go grocery shopping. For them, unlock the door.

Prepare breakfast to be served in bed so they don't wake up.

assist in removing their shoes

After a long day, take them out at random to their preferred restaurant.

Put their suitcase away when they're exhausted following a business trip.

To unwind while on vacation, schedule a massage.

Look after the family and grant them a day off.

Even if it's not your first option, participate in their chosen date activity.

Prepare the bed with fresh linens.

Complete a task they haven't had time to accomplish, like cleaning out the fridge or arranging the cabinets. When they are ill, take care of them. Play their preferred music throughout the house.

Removing the toilet seat

Do one of their tasks, even though it's their turn to do it.

When they're feeling anxious, massage them.

If they have a busy day, pack them a lunch.

Offer to help them move big objects.

.Assist with a project to improve the home

Pick up a treat you enjoy as a surprise.

Remove the dishes without them requesting it.

Shop for groceries.

assist in planning the details of a trip

Get some coffee in the morning.

Cat litter should be cleaned.

Discover their go-to recipe to set up a surprise date.

If it's cold outside, make sure they pack a jacket so they can stay warm.

.Buy supplies of household goods or toiletries in advance before they run out.

Take care of them when they are ill. Play the music of their choice throughout the entire home. Take the toilet seat off

Even though it's their turn to do something, perform one of their responsibilities.

Massage them if they're feeling tense.

Provide them with lunch if they have a busy day.

Offer to assist them in moving heavy items.

assist with a home improvement job

Choose a treat you like to give as a surprise.

Take away the dishes without their permission.

purchase groceries.

aid in making travel arrangements

In the morning, purchase some coffee.

It's important to clean cat litter.

Learn their preferred method for arranging a surprise date.

Make sure they bring a jacket if it's cold so they can stay warm. esteem the tactile, palpable actions you are taking to improve or simplify their lives by giving it a little bit easier. They are able to completely embody their role as a spouse and reciprocate love from a place of abundance when they are not stressed out about the minor but significant things that cause them concern.

Colaku frequently uses the results of the love languages questionnaire in her professional work to aid in communication and understanding between individuals and couples. In order to understand how the other person is feeling, she believes it can be helpful for people to consider how their upbringing, attachment style, and experiences with early caregivers may have impacted their love language. As it allows us to go beyond simply talking about how we want things to be done in the relationship, addressing the love languages is an opportunity to be open with each other, according to her. "We can also explore how we came to think that act of service = being loved."

how to perform a deed of service.

According to psychologist Kira Yakubov, LMFT, "When considering acts of service, think about how you may improve their quality of life by planning ahead or freeing up their time to spend on other things." It demonstrates that you have given thought to their requirements and that you are making efforts to make them smile. This might be as simple as making their coffee to go in the morning to save them a few seconds or as complex as installing jumper cables and a backup battery in their car.

Colaku thinks that it is quite advantageous to enquire about and investigate what they are seeking in particular. "Be mindful and understand what your spouse says they value, what they say they dislike, and how they actually live their daily lives."

dating someone who expresses love via service.

Yakubov offers the following advice for building intimacy with this kind of love language:

1. **ANTICIPATE THEIR REQUIREMENTS CREATIVELY.**

"Keep an eye out for the little things that will improve their day by satisfying a future need of theirs," advises Yakubov. "For example, pack them an umbrella when it might rain or bring snacks to a long event." By considering what they would value, broaden what you can accomplish for them. We run the risk of losing out on what they actually need if we put too much emphasis on carrying out conventional home duties.

2. **KEEP A SHARP EYE OUT AND PAY ATTENTION TO THEIR GRIEVANCES.**

When they have an emotional need, people tend to criticize their partner the loudest. What do you notice they complain about the most if that's the case? How can you offer those areas support?

3. Take into account the skills you naturally possess. They may make a weekly list, which could be useful. Better still, suggests Yakubov, "Ask them what jobs or activities they find challenging or frustrating to identify the areas where you may offer assistance." It's a terrific opportunity to step in if you are specialized or naturally gifted with abilities that your partner lacks to carry out some practical responsibilities.

4. **EXPRESS YOUR GRATITUDE FOR ALL OF THEIR ASSISTANCE.**

"Thank them for helping you by letting them know how much it means to you. Even if their preferred method of receiving love is not verbal affirmation, showing someone you appreciate and recognize what they do can go a long way "she claims. It's always a good idea to try various ways of expressing our love for our mate.

5. **KEEP YOUR PROMISES TO OTHERS.**

They want to know they can rely on their partner to follow through on the pledge since they are so hyper-focused on deeds of service. If it doesn't, people can get angry or dissatisfied. Make sure you follow through on your promise if you accept their request for assistance.

WHAT TO DO IF DEEDS OF SERVICE ARE YOUR LOVE LANGUAGE?

Acts of service are less clear-cut than the other love languages because they heavily depend on your individual experience and your personal priorities. There should be dialogues about expectations that have been met and those that have not been, as observation can only go so far and you can't read each other's minds. Later on, this may help to diffuse underlying tension and conflict.

The partners can check in with one another weekly, bimonthly, or monthly to touch base on how their needs are being addressed by one another and whether they are pleased, according to Colaku. "This is not a one-time dialogue but rather an ever-evolving conversation," she says. Frequent communication is crucial so that couples use the notion of love languages as a springboard for developing a deeper level of fascination with one another rather than as a mechanical method of gaining affection.

THE FINAL RESULT.

These unappealing duties and annoying domestic chores can be transformed into a potent expression of love by being aware of each other's love languages and doing plenty of acts of service.

What occurs in love after marriage?

What happens to love after you are married is a question I have been dying to ask for a very long time.

I inquired, giving up on having a nap, "What do you mean?" He claimed that although each of his three marriages had been great until they were consummated, they had all ended tragically. All of the feelings of love I had for her and that she appeared to have for me vanished. I run a profitable business and consider myself to be reasonably intelligent, yet I don't comprehend it.

How long have you been married? I inquired.

The first one lasted roughly ten years, the second was three years of marriage, and the latest one was close to six years.

Was the loss of your love sudden after the wedding, or did it happen gradually? I questioned.

The second attempt, however, was a complete failure. I have no idea what transpired. I genuinely believed we were in love, but our honeymoon was a complete disaster from which we never fully recovered. We only had a six-month relationship. It was a brief relationship. It was so thrilling! But after the marriage, there was conflict from the start.

We had three or four golden years before the baby arrived in my first marriage. I felt as though she focused all of her attention on the baby after the baby was born, and I was no longer important. She no longer needed me after the pregnancy, as if having children is her only ambition in life.

Oh, I did tell her. She labeled me as crazy. She claimed I didn't get the pressure of working as a nurse around-the-clock. She advised me to show her more compassion and assistance. I made a lot of effort, but nothing seemed to change. We continued to drift apart after that. After some time, all that was left was deadliness instead of love. We both agreed that the marriage was no longer working.

I genuinely believed that my previous marriage would be different. It had been three years after my divorce. We had a two-year relationship. I genuinely believed that we were experts in our field and that, perhaps for the first time, I truly understood what it meant to love someone. She seemed to actually care about me.

I doubt that I changed after the wedding. I still feel the same way about her that I did before we got married. I complimented her on how lovely she was. I expressed my affection to her. I expressed to her my pride in being her husband. However, a few months after we got married, she began griping about small things, like me not taking the trash out or not hanging up my clothing. Later, she turned the conversation to me, accusing me of being unfaithful to her and saying she didn't feel she could trust me. She transformed into a wholly evil individual. Before being married, she was never unfavorable. One of the most upbeat people I've ever encountered was her. One is that. among the factors that drew me to her. She never voiced any complaints. While everything I accomplished was beautiful, it appeared as though I was incapable of doing anything right after we got married. I have no idea what happened. I eventually stopped loving her and started to hate her. She plainly didn't care about me. We came to the conclusion that it was no longer beneficial for us to cohabitate, so we parted ways.

www.ingramcontent.com/pod-product-compliance
Lightning Source LLC
LaVergne TN
LVHW050318160826
845677LV00014B/3465
* 9 7 9 8 8 4 7 3 5 4 2 1 9 *